KOREA
Contrast and Harmony

Editorial, Photo-editing and
Design:
Pacific Media—Korea
President: Richard K. Sink
C.P.O. Box 7630,
Seoul, Korea
Edited by James Wade

Color Separations:
Samhwa Printing Co.
C.P.O. Box 1307,
Seoul, Korea

Phototypesetting:
Daejin Compugraphic
C.P.O. Box 8220,
Seoul, Korea

Printing:
Samsung Moonwha
Printing Co.
C.P.O. Box 4323,
Seoul, Korea

Contributing
Photographers:
Edward Adams, Tom
Chapman, Greg Davis,
Kim Young-eun, Lee Jae-
kyong, Leonard Lueras,
Kevin Orpin, Song Ki-yup

Korean Overseas Information Service
Ministry of Culture and Information
Seoul, Korea

CONTENTS

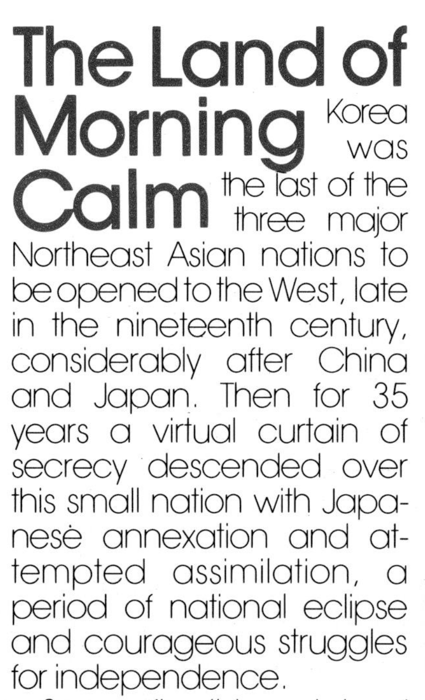

The Land of Morning Calm

Korea was the last of the three major Northeast Asian nations to be opened to the West, late in the nineteenth century, considerably after China and Japan. Then for 35 years a virtual curtain of secrecy descended over this small nation with Japanese annexation and attempted assimilation, a period of national eclipse and courageous struggles for independence.

Soon after this curtain of secrecy lifted with the defeat of Japan at the close of World War II, the Korean War broke out in 1950, bringing about massive destruction and all-pervasive social distuption.

In the late 1950s and later, remarkable things were happening. The rebuilding of wartime damage phased over into a massive economic development program; suddenly Korean products of ever-increasing sophistication were flooding world markets, with an even brighter economic future anticipated.

The ancient "Land of Morning Calm" shows varied faces to a world now waking up to the unique individuality and confident progress of its proud people.

Nature's improvised patterns contrast with the symmetrical designs of man, two opposing poles of the Korean aesthetic experience.

How had this come about so quickly? Those with no inkling of Korea's past, recent or remote, could hardly understand the phenomenon.

A knowledge of Korea's people and their nation—the varied and fascinating arts and artifacts—the stern austerity and melting loveliness of the landscape—is essential for the full understanding of Asian history, and constitutes a continuing source of edifying pleasure as well, in terms of the taut drama these resilient people are still playing out on the stage of their daily lives and in the unfolding pageant of their national history.

For Korea is modern Asia in microcosm: ancient, enduring, patient; yet awakening to recent world trends toward industrialization, social progress, and better lives for all citizens; a traditional society fired by the vision of a finer future; a conservative people moved by overmastering circumstances to seek change or perish; a millennially-old culture coming to terms with the latest innovations, yet clinging tenaciously to its own inner core of values.

These and other aspects of modern Korea make it such a fascinating, revelatory place to study or visit.

기술의 상징
GOLD STAR

KOREA NOW

Korea Now

Today's Korea presents the stimulating, intriguing spectacle of an ancient traditional society emerging rapidly into the modern world, yet preserving the values and ideals that make for social stability and cohesion.

The big cities like Seoul, among the dozen largest metropolises in the world, have the up-to-date cosmopolitan look that one has come to expect: high-rise buildings, broad avenues and busy traffic. But tucked away in unexpected corners one still encounters reminders of a stately and gracious past: old palace compounds dreaming timelessly in the center of town; back alleys of brick-walled houses surmounted by swooping tile roofs; a massive pavilion housing the great bell that used to be rung for the opening and closing of the imposing city gates at morning and evening. Two of the gates still exist marking the modest bounds of the city itself even during this century.

Preceding overleaf, Seoul's imposing skyline rises behind the wooded grounds of an old palace in the foreground.
Seoul at night is a brilliant constellation of lights, a kaleidoscope of vibrant activities, symbolizing the exciting progress the nation has achieved during the past two decades.

기술의상징
GOLD STAR
센타빌딩

The crowded streets of Seoul resound with the sounds of traffic and construction, but a quiet park can always be located for family outings.

The people of Seoul symbolize this blending of the very old and the very new: their assertive, compulsive business drive owes as much to ancient Confucian canons of hard work and self-discipline as to the modern tempo and technology they have so eagerly adopted. But the central core of loyalty to family and friends is still the mainspring of their moral ethos.

And they are friendly, outgoing, gregarious and hospitable in a casual, comfortable way that is quite different from the stereotype of the elusive, inscrutable Oriental once prevalent in the West.

Seoul has seen great changes in its 500 years as Korea's capital, but many vestiges of a proud past remain, treasured by a people with deep roots in ancient traditions.

Change has cast its spell over the faces of the populace too—the vibrant smiles, the frowns of concentration or determination, belong to people who have reared this urban monument to their own aspirations. And the elevation of their morale and confidence had to come, of course, before the material progress it reflects could come to pass.

The National Museum, an imposing new structure designed in a combination of traditional styles, left, stands harmoniously next to ancient buildings in the Kyongbok Palace grounds in Seoul.

Though signs of modernization have spread among a dozen or more smaller Korean cities to a greater or lesser degree, change has not been pursued for its own sake or that of mere novelty, nor have the vestiges of an older, more relaxed era been swept away completely.

Among tangible traces of the past, one still finds in Seoul the three major royal palaces, preserved from dynastic days as public gardens, recreation grounds, and museums, adding their touches of warm color and traditional design to the cosmopolitan cityscape.

Old palaces dream away the decades amidst gardens and foundation stones of vanished buildings in the center of the bustling modern capital.

The Korean Woman

Confucian tradition, strongly entrenched in Korean society over the past 500 years, sternly insisted that woman's place was in the home. This was part of the hierarchical system of dominance and submission on which social order was based: king over subject, father over son, elder over younger, and most definitely husband over wife.

So strong was this ingrained philosophy that during the early phases of modernization 80 years ago, strong objection was raised when Western missionaries set up schools to educate girls.

But the backbone of Confucian resistance was broken in later times of Japanese aggression and the disruptions of the Korean War, when women in various fields of endeavor proved well able to pull their weight in onerous circumstances alongside men.

Actually, Korean women from time immemorial were used to assuming heavy responsibility and acquiring complex skills in the course of household management, where they ruled unchallenged. Many—even queens—pulled strings from behind the scenes to influence their husbands. So the change was not as drastic as it seemed on the surface.

The ways and wiles of past ages are reincarnated in the modern Korean woman.

For a long time, even in modern days, however, a professionally active woman was expected to resign her job upon marriage, on the old assumption that the husband should be ricewinner and the wife kimchi-maker. Women who rejected this theory were unlikely to marry.

Now all that is altering with the prevalence of the nuclear or single-generation family, modern housekeeping aids and especially the ever-increasing numbers of highly-qualified women whose skills—and earning power—are recognized as important assets not only for increased income but also for the prestige of the family, as well as valuable adjuncts to development on the national scale.

Today's women have not forgotten the winsome grace of their ancestresses, but preserve the ancient dress and dances for special occasions.

Cheerful, confident, and competent, Korea's modern woman is contributing her fair share to the nation's modernization and advancement (overleaf).

Young and old, male or female, Koreans dedicate themselves devotedly to sports, whether on the schoolground or in professional events.

The Competitive Spirit

The feverish interest that today's Koreans show in sports derives, perhaps, from the keen competitive spirit which has spearheaded the nation's relentless race toward modernization during the past two decades.

But the urge for athletic excellence was present earlier. A Korean marathon runner won a first-place medal in the 1936 Berlin Olympics. Fired by this example, Koreans have made good showings in international track and field events since the 1950s, and more recently have excelled in basketball, soccer, table tennis, archery and mountaineering on the world sports scene.

The sporting mania starts early, with hard training in school for intramural events that students take with

B.C.KANG
16

80

dead seriousness. Then come the National Athletic Competitions held each fall for the more serious athletes, in effect a selection and elimination contest to pick hot prospects for international contention. The enthusiasm generated by such events makes nearly every Korean an ardent weekend sportsman, sometimes rising at dawn on weekdays too in order to pursue amateur athletics.

Koreans are especially proud that Taekwondo, their own special contribution to the Oriental martial arts, has gained wide popularity in the West, comparable to Japan's karate and China's kungfu.

Enthusiasm, skill, and a fierce competitive spirit characterize Korean athletes of all ages in any game or sporting event.

Youth

For more years than they like to remember, Koreans have had to assume life would be better for their children than it was for themselves. Evidence for such optimism was scant, and in most families such brave dreams seldom came true.

But the hope of any nation must be that its youth will somehow solve, or start unravelling, all the stubborn old problems that elders have failed to straighten out. And now, rather to their surprise, it is happening so swiftly. Koreans are watching a new generation grow up in the 1970s that has every hope, and chance, of enjoying a better life than most of their compatriots have known in this century, or for many centuries past.

Lively young performers in a traditional Korean farmers' dance troupe alternate smiles of satisfaction with expressions of rapt concentration.

(Overleaf) Youthful vim, vitality overflow in the same channels all over the world.

도 신

No wonder such care and affection are lavished upon these youthful standard-bearers, for it is they who will unfurl the banners of a proud if stressful past to the breezes of a promising future.

But love is not equated with license. The young people of Korea, that they may properly enjoy and preserve the nation's progress, grow up under firm discipline, with high family expectations to spur early achievement. And they soon learn that the mature viewpoint of long experience is needed to guide and steady the vigorous steps of the beginner: in the great scales of life, the weight of judicious age must balance that of exuberant youth.

Today's Korean youngsters are always up and doing, developing body and mind to meet the stimulating challenges of the future.

Learning can be fun, modern children discover, carrying on the proud traditions of scholarship established in Korea's distant past.

The foundation of Korean education is a democratic spirit that strives to provide equal opportunity and respect for individual ability. Its purpose, besides providing basic knowledge, is to instill into students the values and skills necessary for building a fully modern nation.

It is the goal of the schools not only to foster creativity but to cultivate values consistent with Korean traditions of filial piety and loyalty to the nation.

The Confucian precept that education is the sole key to future success was deeply ingrained in the Korean spirit. Although modern education was not introduced until 1885, and suffered many adversities during the period of Japanese encroachment and occupation, and in the war that followed liberation, the people have never wavered in this conviction.

While in the past higher education in Korea was largely confined to the liberal arts, the pressing needs of a developing society have created an awareness of both the dignity and the necessity of technical skills, engineering, management, and manual labor. This is reflected in the government policy of encouraging technical and vocational training.

Vocational schools and colleges have been increasing in numbers, size, and sophistication of equipment and curricula.

Well-trained, eager and ambitious graduates of these schools have played a key role in the economic progress of recent years, a vindication of the importance Koreans have always attributed to schooling in both liberal and practical pursuits.

Intent faces reflect the challenge and response of learning

The timeless serenity and wisdom of age dwell upon the faces of these Korean elders, who have earned the trust, the repose and the respect accorded them.

The Age of Respect

In Asian countries such as Korea, the elder still holds an honored status. Elders are treated not only with respect but with loving care, even with some solicitude in regard to their opinions and advice.

The Confucian family system, which still shapes the thinking of most Koreans, gave the highest place to the eldest as head of the family and maker of all decisions. Today's Korean elder may no longer be an absolute autocrat over four generations, as he was a century ago, but neither will he be ignored, treated condescendingly, or sent off to pine away alone in either luxury or penury.

Instead he will be warmly welcomed, hugged to his family's bosom. The warmest spot on the heated floor will be his, the softest bedding, the tenderest morsel from the platter.

For him, indeed, the best is here and now.

To appreciate fully the amazing economic growth of the Republic of Korea, from a pre-industrial agrarian society in 1955 to a modern bastion of sophisticated factories, booming exports and skyrocketing productivity today, it is almost necessary to have visited the devastated, demoralized Korea that was all that was left when the Korean War ended in 1953.

The Economic Miracle

The first priority then was emergency relief, food and medicine for the destitute populace. Then came the task of renewing the sinews of society: chemical fertilizer for farming and increased power generation took precedence.

Next came building the infrastructure for industrialization, including highways, railroads, communications, production of basic consumer goods to ease import needs. Finally heavy industry came on line by the late 1960s.

At left a petrochemical tower silhouetted against the sky; above a freighter delivering raw materials at dockside and right girders erected in construction of a highway overpass—all symbols of Korea's booming economic growth. A panoramic view of the harbor of Pusan (overleaf), Korea's second city and principal port, at night.

These programs were carried out effectively in four successive—and successful—five-year development plans begun in 1962, which rapidly moved the nation into the front ranks of developing, and then of semi-developed countries. In the next phase the nation will begin the "post-industrial" era of advanced countries, where service and information industries tend to predominate.

Even to glimpse so remote a goal after only a quarter century of effort is one more indication of the near-miraculous growth of a revitalized Korea.

The Pohang Iron and Steel Co., lower left, provides the basic material for products such as passenger cars, above, which are fueled by products of the petroleum refineries, right. Industry is powered by Korea's first nuclear reactor, upper left.

Stalwart, hard-working and ambitous, Korean industrial workers report to the factory for another day of toil that will benefit not only their own families but the nation as a whole (overleaf).

The Miracle Workers

Mainspring and catalyst of Korea's economic advance is the Korean worker. Diligent, conscientious, skillful, resourceful and ambitious are words that have been used to describe him; but the single factor that underlies his achievement is that he is well enough educated to aspire successfully to all these other qualities.

Without his basic literacy, moving hand in hand with the age-old "Confucian work ethic" that prods him to toil untiringly for the advancement of his family and nation, Korea's economic miracle could never have taken place. The Korean worker today enjoys a far higher standard of living than he or his father could have imagined 25 years ago.

Fringe benefits of his job include bonuses, meals, health care, on-the-job training in advanced skills, even scholarships for his children. These adjuncts of the Welfare State, however, have not so far sapped his stalwart sense of independence, or blunted his love of the freedom to dream his own dreams and carve out his own future.

As long as he retains this degree of independence and initiative, the future of the economy which his energies fuel so effectively would seem secure.

The individual is the basis of Korea's economic advance, for the nation has few of the raw materials necessary for modern industry. In effect, it is exporting the accumulated expertise of its workers.

Strength

Throughout nearly 5,000 years of history, the Korean peninsula has been a focal point for rivalry—political, economic and territorial. This has resulted in hundreds of foreign invasions and incursions, long and short, large and small.

In order to preserve national integrity and protect cultural independence, Koreans have had to rally their combined strength time and again—not only for regular military operations, but in the guerrilla warfare waged by Buddhist monks harrassing Hideyoshi's marauders during the 1590s.

Today, no less than then, Koreans are firmly united and stubbornly determined in standing together to insure the nation's survival, whatever the perils and sacrifices they may face.

Ever ready to repel any renewed attack from North Korea, the Republic's military might parades each October 1 on Armed Forces Day.

THE PAST

The Past

The present is a moving point of no dimension, dividing past from future, some philosophers say. We cannot discern the future, and we can only fleetingly perceive the present. Therefore much of what we know derives from the past; but this can help us interpret the present and plan for the future.

Korea is a country with a long past—too much past, it is sometimes said. Yet Koreans have a legitimate pride in that past, and in recent years, rather than dwelling on its glories and disasters too nostalgically, have begun learning to use their knowledge of what has already occurred to illuminate the present and the future.

This gives a sense of continuity to Korean life, and buttresses the stability of traditions.

It is good to know of one's roots, certainly; it is even better to water those roots now, and look forward to the rich havest of fruit and grain tomorrow. And this seems to be the Korean way.

A warrior general from the proud past, left, seems to lead the advance into a brighter future. An elder, right, explains the meaning of a patriotic bas relief to visitors at a public park.

The Greatest Hero

Korea was militarily unprepared when Japanese forces of the warlord Hideyoshi struck across the narrow strait separating the two countries in 1592. Hastily marshalled Korean armies could not hold against the invaders, who were equipped with rifles.

On the seas, however, Korea produced her own defender in the person of Adm. Yi Sun-shin, who employed newly-improved "turtle boats," the world's first ironclad warships, to scour the seas of Japanese vessels and thus break the invader's lifeline for supplies and reinforcements.

The Japanese withdrew, defeated. When Hideyoshi struck at Korea again in 1597, Adm. Yi again defeated the Japanese navy and thwarted Hideyoshi's invasion scheme.

But after directing several tactically brilliant battles, Adm. Yi was struck down by a sniper's bullet at the moment of victory on the deck of his flagship.

Koreans still revere his name as the greatest military hero and patriot of the nation.

Modern paintings bring to vivid life the career of Adm. Yi, heroic 16th century military leader and inventor of the world's first ironclad warship, the turtle boat.

The Korean War, which began on June 25, 1950, with a surprise attack on the unprepared South by

The Korean War

overwhelmingly superior forces from the Communist North, was a direct result of the ill-advised division of the nation after Japan's defeat in World War II.

Moreover, the fanatical northern regime—encouraged and equipped by Stalin—schemed to take over the entire peninsula. Their sudden onslaught was blunted and reversed by expeditionary forces dispatched by sixteen United Nations members after the Security Council approved the intervention.

But Communist China sent its forces into the fray, resulting in an eventual stalemate along approximately the old line of division.

Truce talks dragged on in the midst of bloody if inconclusive fighting until a fragile armistice, which still continues, was signed on July 27, 1953.

The most lasting damages from the Korean War though—still felt today—was the hardening of the division and animosity between south and north Koreans.

American General Douglas MacArthur, left, accepts the flag of the United Nations Command during his momentous service in the Korean War of 1950. A refugee child sits despondently amid the ruins of Seoul, above right, during the Communist invasion.
Refugees flee in panicky confusion, right, as Communist forces approach during the early days of the 1950 Korean War.

THE LAND

The Land

Korea is a mountain-riven land with a rugged natural beauty that has inspired her artists and fascinated her people since ages past.

Her mountains, while not lofty, rise steep and jagged from the plains, assuming monumental proportions and shedding from their granite peaks the drenching rains and melting snows in the form of short, torrential rivers.

Squeezed in, as it were, between towering ranges, the central plains—though broader to the south—must be farmed with unrelenting intensity in order to provide enough grain for the dense population. Even steep hillsides are cultivated in places where human foothold seems precarious at best.

Preceding overleaf, level farm fields fill the valleys before a backdrop of Korea's ever-present mountains.
White blankets enshroud Korea's uplands and mountains as winter's wizardry enchants the rugged landscape.
Overleaf, a craggy snow-streaked peak overlooks a range of lesser mountains in the warmth of morning sunlight.

The climate is temperate, much milder than in Siberian latitudes to the north. The winters, though often cold, tend to be dry, without much snowfall except at high altitudes. Two cold days are said always to be followed by three warmer ones, and the pattern usually holds true.

The main precipitation occurs in July and August, when seasonal monsoons lash the peninsula and dump almost daily rains into an atmosphere that is already steamily oppressive. Rushing streams deepen and widen, and there is always danger of floods.

The misty, tree-clad slopes of Korean mountain ranges bloom with vibrant colors when leaves turn in the autumn. (Overleaf) A craggy, snow-sprinkled peak rises over surrounding ranges and valleys in a winter panorama.

Overleaf, fogs produce pastel tints in an early-morning landscape.

The short, mild springtime and the long, hazily warm autumns are the most pleasant seasons in Korea, as evidenced not only in the subject matter of ancient poets, but by the migration patterns of today's holiday makers, who stream out of the cities every weekend to seek rural recreation whenever the weather permits.

Fields of oil-seed flowers create a brilliant rural tapestry in spring, left, as cherry tree blossoms emblazon the landscape with lacy filigree.
Overleaf, winter sportsmen are dwarfed by the blinding white expanses of the slopes down which they ski.

RURAL LIFE

The Rural Life

Rural folk everywhere are considered conservative and slow to adapt. But Korea's farmers in recent years have happily supported changes that led to higher income and living standards, lower rates of disease and malnutrition, easier access to transportation, communication and education. These changes have broken down most of the barriers between the country and city dweller: as a matter of fact, average rural household income has surpassed that of urban blue-collar families.

But in the countryside some things do not change.

Farmers and fisher-folk still follow a seasonal pattern of preparation, cultivation, and garnering. The seasons stay the same, but as they pass, human life is enriched and emancipated to enjoy the immemorial cycle.

Preceding overleaf, elders in traditional costume pace beside their farm fields past a strawstack adorned with squash vines.

Korea is a land of distinct seasons and a timeless rural cycle of planting, cultivation and harvest. At left, blossoming cherry trees in spring overhang a greening rice field. In summer, workers take time off to consume some of their melon harvest, above, and an old man contemplates the rich autumn harvest with quiet satisfaction, above right.

Overleaf, farm women carry produce to market over country roads as the sun rises over the rugged rural countryside.

Those who plow and harvest the seas perform just as vital a function as the grain farmers, for fish provide an essential part of the nation's protein intake.

Like their brothers on land, the fishermen are experiencing the benefits of modernization of equipment and techniques which adds to their income and output.

Laden fishnets announce the tidings of a successful day at sea, left, while a fisherman's family greets his return, right.

Overleaf, colorful fishnets are laid out to dry before the next day at sea.

지리 2.

Saemaul

Koreans have always had to work hard; while circumstances dictated the necessity of working together. Out of these facts arose the threefold slogan of the Saemaul: diligence, cooperation and self-help.

Saemaul is the Korean name for the New Community Movement which has played a key role in elevating the living standards of the rural populace to equal and then exceed those of the newly-affluent urban wage earners. Since its conception by the late President Park in 1971, it has also proved effective in alleviating urban problems and smoothing labor-management relations, making Korea a model country in the developing world for phased progress benefitting all strata of society.

This voluntary self-help system, with minimal government guidance and support plus maximum rice-roots participation in planning and decision-making, has rapidly instilled a vital new spirit in Koreans that has worked wonders during a short span of time in renovating farm, home, factory and neighborhood.

Ancient, laborious methods of irrigation have given way to modern reservoirs and aqueducts as part of the Saemaul or New Community Movement.

Overleaf, seaside women head for market in the mists of early morning.

CULTURE AND THE ARTS

Culture and the Arts

Korean culture, like Korean food, has a special flavor of its own that is unmistakable after even a single sampling; a unique savor that transforms even the simplest ideas or ingredients into something special, though it may not appeal to every palate.

It is true enough to say that the initial stimulus for much of Korean literature, music, and art came from China; still, something distinctive always emerged eventually. And of course the further back the continental influence, the more its peninsular reflection departs from the original with the passage of time.

To deal in generalities before specifics, Korean art is intuitive and spontaeous, intriguingly imperfect, modest and subtle, unlike that of the Chinese empire, which tended to be massive, perfectly polished, and perhaps a bit cold and remote.

Thus Korea's transitional peninsular art stands midway between the continental ideal of China and the island ideal of Japan, combining, perhaps, some of the best features of both.

Preceding overleaf, a girl in graceful traditional costume evokes memories of an ancient culture, playing the kayagum in gracious old-style surroundings. Graceful dancers in bright costumes perform the Flower Crown Dance, left. An ancient Buddhist image with damaged aureole is decorated with flame-like patterns, above right.

Court musicians, left, perform upon the kayagum and komungo, two types of Korean zither, and at right, the piri, a double reed oboe.

Korean Music

The sound is both nasal and shrill; slow, long-held notes dissolving into lacy decorative arabesques, punctuated by the single thump of a drum, one pungent stroke of gong or chime or cymbal.

The tones, as they move with solemn decorum to outline vast arching melodies, sound strangely piquant—this is not the Western scale of piano keyboards and symphony orchestras, with the same mathematical ratio between adjacent tones, but a gapped, gamier scale, with different distances between pitches, and a subtler selectivity in deciding how many notes to use, and when.

It is music considered as adjunct to a religious ritual, or a solemn official ceremony, colorful but dignified.

Before the tempered scale, before the keyboard or the viol, before organum or Gregorian chant, these musicians of old Korea, clad in their bright but stately robes, have been wafting their subtle, serene melodies in the trembling air; and perhaps will still be doing so when the impatient modern generation has gone on to seek newer, but not necessarily better, musical novelties.

Dance

Dignity and grace balanced by acrobatic vigor—these are the two poles of Korean traditional dance.

The first is characteristic of the ancient ceremonial court dances performed at royal ceremonies and celebrations. But their solemnity is spiced with subtle beauties of hue and movement, with an elusive charm, an ethereal repose, lending them aesthetic as well as spiritual elevation.

Court ladies stepped the patterns of these languid or spirited dances for the edification of royalty and nobility. Their costumes of bright or pastel silk, long-skirted and full-sleeved, had to be as perfect as their elaborate coiffures, each thread and hair in place, each nod and twirl and gesture impeccable.

It was an aristocratic art, created by and for the connoisseur.

Not so the folk dances of the farmers, improvised for such rural festivals as those of planting and harvest times, but carrying forward a tradition at least as ancient and elaborate as the court dance.

Korean dance partakes of both the earthy and the airy in its blend of exuberance and discipline.

Overleaf, the masked dances of the rural peasantry were usually satiric in content, such as this earthy drama depicting an apostate Buddhist monk on the left attempting to seduce a country maiden.

Farmers' Dance

The farmers' dance was as fast and furious as the court ladies' was slow and sedate.

The costumes were simpler but the rhythms more complex, the movements almost acrobatic in their complexity.

What musicians call polyrhythms, and strive to write down in our inadequate modern notation, had the dancer's feet moving deftly in patterns completely ignoring, or defying, the intricate beat of drums and clatter of gongs.

There was sweat in these dances, but an infinite sense of elation too.

A fleeting flash of white—straw sandals shuffling in the dust, competing against complex cross-rhythms of drum, gong and bugle; a slithering of airborne paper streamers from the crown of a wildly gyrating headdress; wild acrobatics mounting in a crescendo of frenzy: this is the Korean farmers' dance, a community orgy of seasonal triumph over nature at the immemorial times of planting and harvest.

The serene wisdom of the Confucian scholar-administrator is reflected in this court portrait from the mid-Yi Dynasty, left.
Coiled power in repose emanates from the tiger in a Yi Dynasty painting, below. A fantastic landscape overshadows faint traces of human habitation in a Yi Dynasty folding screen, of which this is one panel, right.
(Overleaf) A map of Seoul's old Changdok Palace compound becomes an intriguing work of art on this folding screen from the Yi Dynasty.

Painting

Tomb murals from the Koguryo Kingdom, prior to the seventh century, are the earliest extant Korean paintings.

Not until the Yi Dynasty, around the 15th century, are there enough additional extant paintings to generalize about.

There were then two classes of artist: professionals employed by the royal court for portraits, decorative landscapes, and genre paintings; and amateurs, actually highly-cultivated scholar-poets who would never have demeaned themselves by selling or exhibiting their art works.

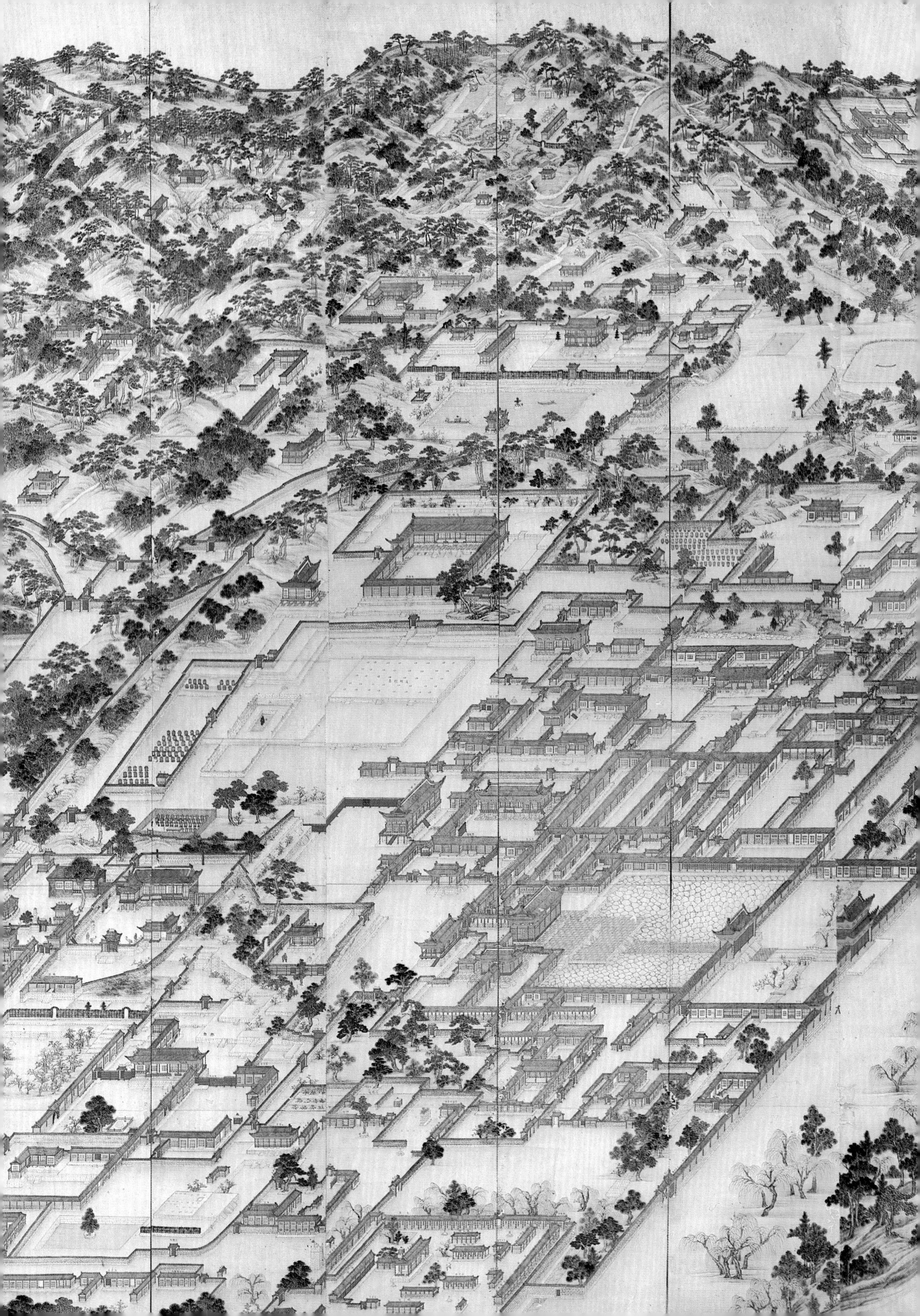

The supporting pillar, pediment, rafters and eaves of a traditional building are carved and painted into a bewildering complexity of colors and designs in the tanchong style of decoration, embodying good luck and protective symbols for the building and its inhabitants.

Tanchong

Tanchong means, literally, "red and blue," but there are many more shades and hues involved in this art of decorating the exposed woodwork both inside and outside traditional Korean buildings. Palaces, temples, shrines, Confucian schools and other official buildings, all were emblazoned with these dazzling painted designs on rafter, ceiling and eaves.

The art of tanchong is very old, having been traced back at least 1,500 years, and the employment of specific design motifs was once governed by elaborate rules and undertaken for quite specific purposes, though little of this tradition remains, perhaps, to undergird the work of today's artisans.

In the words of one recent writer: "Under the simple tiled roofs, a world of flowers, animals and auspicious symbols was created. For those whose eyes turn upward in prayer, in thought or in joy and wonder, tanchong's laughing rainbow is to be seen."

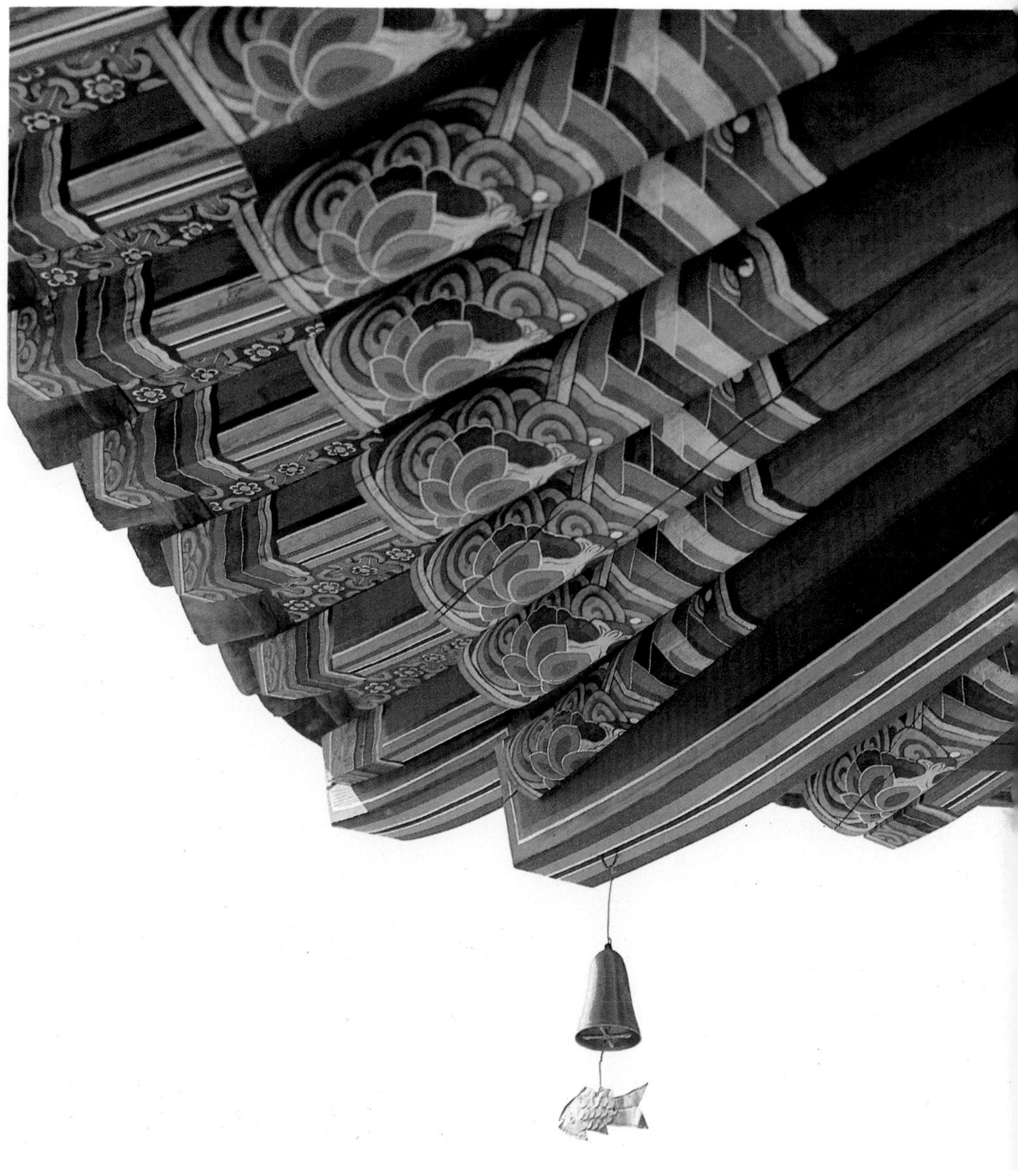

Literature

The earliest surviving Korean writings are poems and histories handed down from Koryo times a thousand years ago, long before the invention of the Hangul alphabet, and thus written entirely in Chinese ideographs used phonetically.

By late Koryo times, 600 or more years past, the brief lyric verse form called sijo had been devised. At first sijo were always chanted to musical background, but later became a purely literary form, vehicle for the expression of a characteristic gamut of Korean feelings, from nostalgia and nature evocation to love and political satire.

Novels appeared by the middle years of the Yi Dynasty, in or before the 18th century. The most popular of them embodied elements of social satire or reformist ideals, as in Hong Kildong, the story of a Korean Robin Hood who rebelled against the social stigma inherent in his status as son of a secondary wife; or Chunhyangjon, in which a lowborn girl of the entertainer class remains faithful to her absent aristocrat husband, defying a corrupt and lecherous magistrate.

The scholar's cabinet, left, contains all the paraphernalia of literature: books, scrolls, paper, brush, ink paints, inkstone, water jars; even spectacles to ease any resultant eye-strain.

Bindings of old Korean books, above, written in Chinese, and part of a specimen page of text, exemplifying the high regard in which literary scholarship was held during the Yi Dynasty.

The most outstanding of the many cultural and practical achievements of Korea's 15th century "Confucian humanist" monarch, King Sejong the Great, was the invention by a com-

Hangul

mittee of scholars under direct royal supervision of the Korean phonetic alphabet called Hangul, a system still in use today, which has given Korea one of the highest literacy rates in the world.

Before Sejong's time, Korea—like many Asian countries within the sphere of China's cultural influence—had used complex Chinese ideographs.

Sejong's experts devised a simple phonetic system of 26 letters that accurately represented all the vowels and consonants of Korean. Though the system was not widely adopted until the 20th century, today it is universally utilized, with Chinese ideographs employed, if at all, only for proper names and abstract concepts.

King Sejong's 500-year-old inspiration thus continues to benefit his posterity today, the heritage of a truly enlightened ruler.

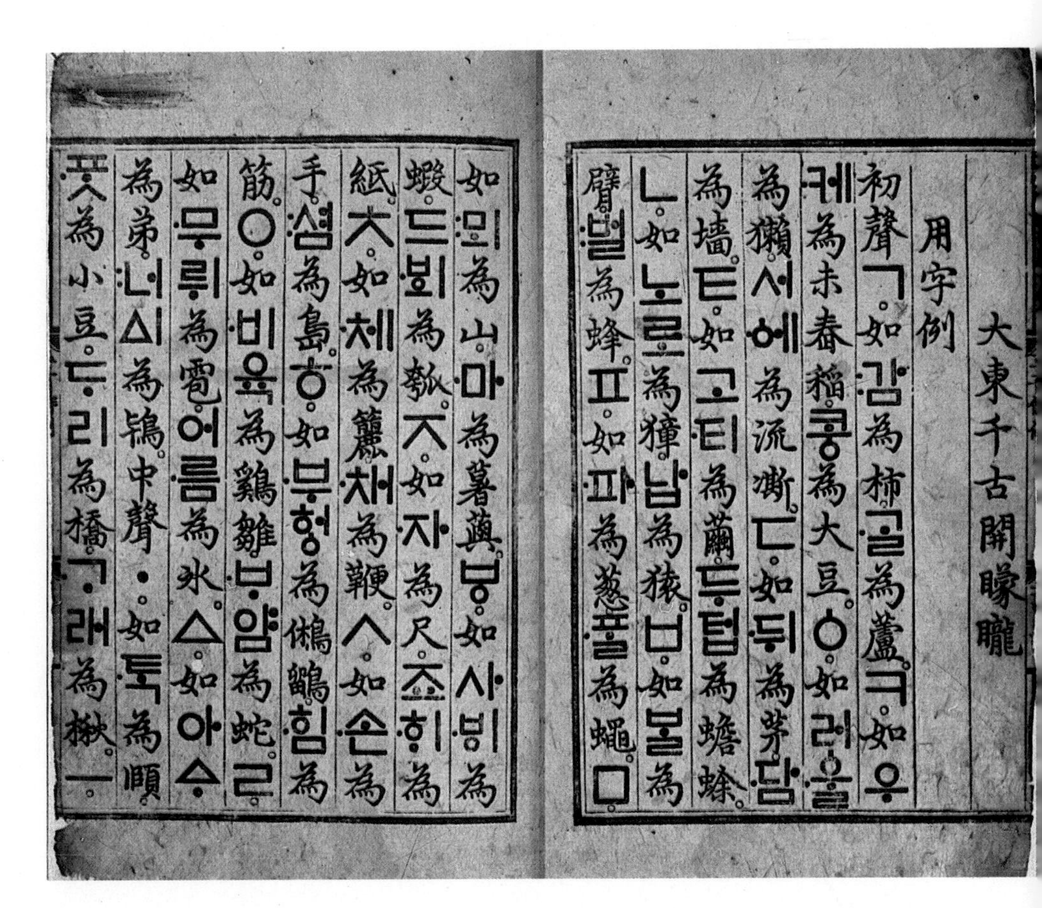

大東千古開曚曨

用字例

初聲ㄱ如감爲柿골爲蘆ㅋ如우
케爲未舂稻콩爲大豆ㆁ如러ᇰ울
爲獺서에爲流凘ㄷ如뒤爲茅담
爲墻ㅌ如고티爲繭두텁爲蟾蜍
ㄴ如노로爲獐납爲猿ㅂ如볼爲
臂벌爲蜂ㅍ如파爲葱ᄑᆞᆯ爲蠅ㅁ

如뫼爲山마爲薯藇ᄫ如사ᄫᅵ爲
蝦드ᄫᅴ爲瓠ㅈ如자爲尺죠ᄒᆡ爲
紙ㅊ如체爲籭채爲鞭ㅅ如손爲
手셤爲島ㆆ如부헝爲鵂鶹힘爲
筋ㅇ如비육爲鷄雛ᄇᆞ얌爲蛇ㄹ
如무뤼爲雹어름爲氷ㅿ如아ᅀᆞ爲
弟너ᅀᅵ爲鴇中聲ㆍ如ᄐᆞᆨ爲頤
ᄑᆞᆺ爲小豆ᄃᆞ리爲橋ᄀᆞ래爲楸ㅡ

The 80,000-odd carved wooden printing plates for Buddhist scriptures, one of the most impressive monuments of Koryo Dynasty culture, are still usable after nearly 800 years. They are stored in this warehouse at Haein-sa Temple, left.

An early specimen of printing using the Korean alphabet, Hangul, invented during the 15th century, interspersed with Chinese characters to explicate the then-unfamiliar phonetic letters, above right.

The unglazed grey Silla Dynasty pottery jars, left, contrast with Yi Dynasty glazed porcelain with inlaid designs, lower left, and Koryo celadon ware below and Yi Dynasty porcelain bottle, right.

Ceramics

Korean ceramics, especially the blue-green glazed celadon pottery of the Koryo Dynasty produced a thousand and more years ago, are by far the most famous class of art objects the nation has achieved. Long valued and sought after in the West not only for beauty but for fine craftsmanship, Koryo celadon can be imitated but not duplicated today.

The composition and tint of the glaze and the secrets of the firing technique were forgotten as early as the succeeding Yi Dynasty, whose pottery was primarily white porcelain with underglaze designs in pale blue or rust red. This was sufficiently admired that invading Japanese armies in 1592-8 kidnapped Korean potters to begin Japan's fine ceramics industry.

The earlier grey unglazed pots decorated with geometrical "comb patterns" produced by Silla and the Three Kingdoms have their admirers too, who favor their rude simplicity and grace above more sophisticated products.

Among Korea's national treasures, none rank higher than the exquisite Buddhist devotional images in metalwork produced by artists of ancient times.

National Treasures

Any nation with a long history gradually accumulates a variety of art objects and artifacts that constitute the core of its cultural heritage; and Korea, with a known history stretching back thousands of years, is especially well-endowed in this respect. As in several other Asian countries, the government here has designated a number of these ancient objects as National Treasures in order that their importance may be recognized, and steps taken to protect and preserve them, as well as to draw public and scholarly attention in suitable directions.

Many of Korea's most ancient relics are of a religious nature, products of the Golden Age of Buddhism during the Silla and Koryo Dynasties. Others constitute objects taken from ancient tombs or other archaeological excavations.

Dating from much more recent times are painted screens and scrolls, portraits, and albums of genre pictures—delicate and perishable objects whose predecessors perished from fire, age or neglect.

Prominent among these remains of the past are celadon and porcelain ceramic masterpieces of the last thousand and more years.

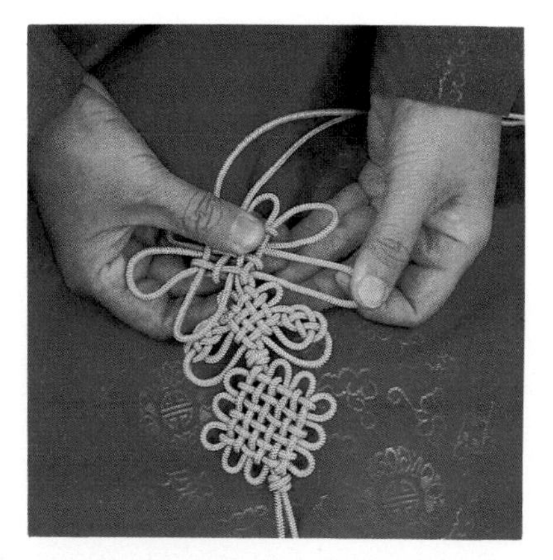

Living Treasures

Not all of a nation's cultural heritage resides in static objects made of wood, metal, stone, clay or cloth. Much of it is embodied in human beings and their skills.

The craftsmanship required to create some artifact of lacquer, wood or bamboo; furniture, accessories, musical instruments; the physical dexterity and discipline needed to play a game or perform a dance: these qualities are cultivated, utilized, conserved and conveyed to disciples by Korea's unique "Living National Treasures."

Their numbers may be small, their eminence little known in today's busy modern world; but the official recognition and support they have earned insures that the vital spark of creativity they nurture within themselves will not entirely perish.

Braiding and fancy knot work for costume decoration of court dress and the clothing of aristocrats, left, was a highly specialized craft that has almost disappeared today, practiced only by a few dedicated traditional woman artisans.

Festival

Every so often comes a day when bright traditional costumes are brought out for airing, when rice cakes are washed down with rice wine; when old games, sports and contests are revived for the occasion by people whose everyday hectic schedule is temporarily relaxed.

Korean festivals may be national in scale, like the annual Folk Arts Contest; regional, like the varied and colorful pageants staged to commemorate important historical events; local, like the farmers' carnivals held at times of spring planting and fall harvest; or strictly family, as in the elaborate parties for a child's hundredth day or an elder's sixtieth year.

Large or small, general or special, a Korean celebration is always something special, partaking of both ritual and revelry.

Fireworks bloom in brilliant flame over the city to herald the gala Silla Festival, right, in the ancient capital of Kyongju. Koreans are always ready and enthusiastic participants in any party or celebration, large or small.

Buddha's Birthday

The most recent national holiday added to the Korean calendar is Buddha's Birthday, in belated recognition of the continuing influence which Buddhism has exerted on the peninsula since its introduction over 1,500 years ago from China and India.

Twelve million Koreans claim adherence to this religion, making it the largest single organized faith, so its influence is widespread. Temples large and small dot the countryside, many of them enshrining sacred relics of saints and sages, and housing historical and artistic treasures.

Glowing lanterns, serenely smiling images usher in Buddha's birthday, one of the most festive holidays on the calender.

The austere interior of a Christian cathedral—the bulbous dome of a Muslim mosque—the colorful ancient costumes for a Confucian rite—symbolize the varieties of religious experience available to Koreans.

Faith

Korea's religions have not only built up in layers over the ages, they have penetrated and mixed with one another like the blended tints of an Impressionist painting.

The basic undercoating of the picture is primitive animism—a worship of spirits inherent in a specific place or object.

Over this background were superimposed the bold, bright figures of Buddhist creed, the strict formal outlines of Confucian ethics and the subtle, elusive hues of Taoism's nature mysticism for contrast.

All four systems of belief, developed or imported before the fifth century A.D., still exist, and each has profoundly influenced the others in terms of creed, ritual and philosophy, although laymen and ordinary believers are usually not consciously aware of such amalgamations.

Meanwhile, Christianity had entered the picture, less than a century ago to

any significant extent, but looming large in the foreground through its identification with modern education, Western values, and international technology.

Korea embraces many creeds, but has no state religion; freedom of belief is guaranteed by the Constitution and upheld in practice. Thus the Koreans can reshape and alter the composition of this varied religious picture as they please, and as they always have done.

Buddhist temple life embraces a multiplicity of work, study and devotion.

Overleaf, vast bas relief carvings of Buddhist saints epitomize the long tradition of Korea's arts.

DISCOVERING
KOREA

Discovery

Discovering Korea as a world travel destination has been the exciting experience of a million or more foreign travellers per year, beginning in 1978, when the nation became the seventh country in Asia to reach the goal of attracting one million visitors annually.

This came as the climax to a decade of rapid development during which Korea's tourist arrivals grew at an average annual rate of more than 30 percent.

Preceding overleaf, travellers faintly glimpsed in morning mist set off on an exciting pilgrimage to discover Korea.
Two ancient Buddhist pagodas are reflected in a pool at sunset. At right, huge Buddha images called Miroks are carved from the living granite of a hillside near Seoul. (The small image is a modern addition.)
Overleaf, fishing and ferry boats thread their way between capes and islands in the turqoise seas of Korea's Hallyo Waterway.

Hotel Shilla

Hospitality

After the tourist arrives—attracted by effective overseas promotion, and wafted effortlessly on his way by convenient transport scheduling—he must have a comfortable place to stay, a reassuring place to eat, ease in getting around and finding out what he needs to know and most of all a wide selection of things to see, do and buy to divert the time of his stay pleasantly.

Korea qualifies handily in all departments. Especially remarkable has been the recent proliferation of top-class hotels meeting the highest international standards.

Modern design and superlative facilities characterize Korea's luxury hotels.

SEOUL PLAZA HOTEL
경축 제57회 어린이날 어린이대행진
HYATT

The first of these international hotels—many of them foreign-invested or managed—opened less than a decade ago, but today there are nearly a dozen, including several in resort areas remote from Seoul.

By precept and example, they are setting standards that elevate the service and facilities offered by their closest competitors.

What they offer in terms of luxury accommodations, stylish decor, fine food and drink, deluxe shopping, and sophisticated recreation challenges comparison with similar institutions in any nation of the Asia-Pacific region.

Towering new hotels punctuate Seoul's skyline, offer gracious living to visitors.

Overleaf, Korea's lavish new resort complex at Kyongju was site of the Pacific Area Travel Association (PATA) workshop following the 1979 conference in Seoul.

KYONGJU CHOSUN
PATA DELEGATES
WELCOME

TA79
REA
ANNUAL WORKSHOP
JU CHOSUN HOTEL

Korean food is one of the pleasantest discoveries the neophyte traveller will make during his visit here.

Korea's unique cuisine is another aspect of the nation's distinctively different culture; neither its ingredients nor its seasonings resemble dishes of any other country, near or far.

Korean Fare

Most Korean foods are boldly spiced, carrying the blended tang and savor of red pepper, garlic, onions or leeks, sesame seed and oil, and soy sauce. However, the flavoring can be subltle too in delicate soups, regal casseroles, fragrant whte rice and all the special dishes based on rice, including decorative rice cakes for special occasions.

Among the most popular dishes are—besides ever-present white rice—the spicy fermented cabbage kimchi and the tangy barbecued beef strips known as Bulgogi, cooked at the table on charcoal braziers.

A left-over from the royal kitchen is the elaborate Kujolpan table, a banquet in itself, in which intriguing fillings are mixed and rolled up in tiny pancakes like miniature tortillas. Not found everywhere, but a dish fit for a king.

Korean foods range from the bland to the blistering: peppery kimchi, delicate stews and soups, intriguingly seasoned side dishes of vegetable, fish or meat, and the royal banquet, above right, known as Kujolpan.

Scenic Korea

In the matter of scenic attractions, nature and history have endowed this compact nation with more than its share of blessings per square mile.

Rugged mountains, rushing rivers, fragrant forests and fertile fields form backdrops to peaceful temples, imposing palaces, and stimulating recreation grounds. The big cities offer cosmopolitan facilities and activities as well, but it is in outlying areas that visitors can savor the real essence of what Korea is all about. More and more travellers are hitting the trail to Korea's fabulous countryside, seeking this elusive but elating discovery.

Modern transportation links scenic spots in a network characterized by speed and convenience.

A train crosses a railway trestle over tidal flats as day draws to a close. (overleaf)

Korea's mountains often make up in steepness and ruggedness for their relative lack of height. This is

Mount Sorak

the case especially at Mt. Sorak National Park on the northeast coast, where towering escarpments resemble the battlements of fantastic castles.

Often thick mists drift around and between the peaks, blurring outlines and smudging steep distant pine woods into figures from an old ink scroll picture.

Here, in fact, is where ancient artists received their inspiration for those treasured paintings, the subjects of which seem imaginatively extravagant to those who have not visited Sorak.

Only five hours from Seoul by bus or car, a resort is under development here which offers not only traditional pursuits like hiking and mountain-climbing, but also the conveniences of luxury hotels, international cuisine, swimming or skiing in season.

The Mt. Sorak National Park is large enough so that even after completion of the resort there will be many acres of unspoiled wilderness remaining to intrigue the nature-lover, excite the sportsman and inspire the photographer or artist to emulate the masterpieces of the past.

Autumn colors are sometimes muted by the mists that form around the craggy peaks of Mt Sorak.

(Overleaf) Rock-strewn streams drain melting snows in Mt. Sorak National Park.

Cheju Island

Even for those who know Korea well, the island province of Cheju is something else.

Awash in green and violet seas far to the south of the peninsula, its climate is almost tropical, with citrus fruits and exotic blossoms flourishing—its landscape is nearly lunar, strewn with pitted boulders and slabs of black basalt spewed up by volcanic action millions of years past.

It has been called the island of rocks, wind, and women; and traditionally lacks thieves, beggars and gates. It is also a place where stalwart women dive to dizzying depths undersea to harvest shellfish and seaweed.

Whatever else Cheju may be, one is safe in saying: It's different.

Cheju Island presents contrasting vistas of blooming flowers, beating surf, and plunging waterfalls against a backdrop of stark black volcanic basalt rocks.

Kyongju

This sleepy rural town in southeastern Korea is fast awakening to new celebrity as a vacation resort and archaeological treasure trove.

But it has a long way to go to equal its past glories as capital of the Silla Kingdom that unified all Korea in 636 A.D.

In those palmy days, Kyongju held a million citizens in secure comfort or relative luxury, attracting traders from as far away as India and Arabia, erecting magnificent palaces, temples and royal tombs whose impressive remains fascinate today's swarming tourists, casting the largest and loveliest bronze bell in the Orient, and building Asia's largest observatory for star study, both still existing and admired.

The cultural efflorescence lasted less than three centuries, after which Silla fell, the capital of the new kingdom was moved and Kyongju went to sleep for a thousand years. With its awakening, visitors can again glimpse the dreams of past glory that haunted that millennial slumber.

Upper left, a massive serene statue of Buddha dominates the mountaintop stone grotto shrine called Sokkuram at Kyongju.
Left, ancient royal tomb mounds in Tumulus Park, Kyongju, recall the glorious days of the Silla Dynasty,
Right, the Emille Bell, largest cast bronze bell in the Orient, adorns the grounds of Kyongju's National Museum branch.